JAME

Health & Wellbeing for Men

How to invest in yourself with 81 wellbeing and self care habits

First published by RJM Publishing 2022

Copyright © 2022 by James Armstrong

All rights reserved. No part of this publication may be reproduced, stored or transmitted in any form or by any means, electronic, mechanical, photocopying, recording, scanning, or otherwise without written permission from the publisher. It is illegal to copy this book, post it to a website, or distribute it by any other means without permission.

First edition

This book was professionally typeset on Reedsy.
Find out more at reedsy.com

Contents

Special Bonus	iv
Introduction	1
Prioritizing to Include You	5
How to Find That Work-Life Balance	9
Starting New Hobbies	16
Making Time for You	21
How Can Mindfulness Help?	29
Health the Holistic Way	39
Home Work Out	43
Improving Sleep and Stress	51
How to Benefit from Embracing Creativity	56
Give and Take	60
What Difference do People (and Animals) Make?	64
Do it Your Way!	74
And Finally	82

Special Bonus

Get this bonus Believe it and Achieve it book absolutely **free!**

Plus access to other free health, fitness, self care and well-being books and guides by joining the James Armstrong Book Club.

Download here

Introduction

In this book, I will share 81 habits, tools, and techniques for living a happier, healthier and more fulfilled life. These are strategies successfully used by people from all walks of life, from busy senior executives managing complex work and balancing active home lives to people fresh to the employment market, new parents, and retired seniors.

Being content and feeling fulfilled is something that we all want. But, too often, the hustle and bustle of day-to-day activities get in the way. Use this guide to learn, step by step, how to put your well-being first, improve your health, and achieve long-lasting happiness.

We invest time and effort in so many things, helping members of our families and friends, building careers and businesses, teaching others, and learning. However, your level of success in such things depends on your one biggest asset and how well it is functioning - YOU!

We all know that before helping someone else put their oxygen mask on, we must put on our own first. The same applies to investing in yourself. By following the steps in this book and improving your physical and mental well-being, you automatically enhance things for those you love and support too. So read on...

How to use this book

This book is crammed full of tips and techniques that people have successfully used to make their lives happier and more fulfilled.

You can use this book in different ways, but I recommend that you pick out, as you read, a number of initial changes to focus on. These can be things that might be easier to embrace, or that you know will bring you the most positive impact, or they might just feel enjoyable.

Use this selection as your first set of goals to help you to get started quickly and easily with making changes. Then, once you have made these initial changes, you can move on to make the next set of changes, and so on.

You will find that this set-by-step approach gives you a great start. Your first set of goals can very quickly change your life for the better. So as you read, why not note which ideas you plan to begin with, and make some immediate changes, to start your journey towards a happier, healthier you today.

Fighting the stigma

When talking about men's mental health and well-being, it's no big news that there exists a lot of stigma surrounding it. So it's only natural that we address this first because most of the time, when men fail to administer proper self-care for themselves, it is because of these stigmas.

Our society already has a very narrow view of mental health. Talking about one's personal issues is not something our society always accepts welcomingly, but it's even more difficult for men.

No matter what part of the world you're from, you've probably heard some

INTRODUCTION

version of "men need to be strong and stoic". That is how, in fact, most people expect men to behave. Men are often expected to be always dependable, in control, physically strong, and most importantly, self-reliant.

There's a reason for these expectations. Historically, men have most commonly been the provider of the family. Even as far back as the times of the hunter-gatherers, men did the hunting while women took other duties, such as gathering resources, tending to the young, and so on. Even today, this system persists in most parts of the world. About 74-75% of households in the USA and UK have men as the primary breadwinner.

Another side of the same problem is that since our society pushes these expectations on men, most men, especially those who have lived a significant part of their life handling their own problems, see mental health issues as something they can address by themselves. Some men even see considering their mental health as a sign of weakness and thus disregard it altogether. This kind of thinking hinders men from getting the help they need and can develop over time into something more dangerous such as toxic masculinity. "I'm just sad. I'll go out, have a beer, take a walk, and I'll be fine again." – This is the type of internal conversation that men sometimes use to justify not talking about their problems. Have you ever found yourself in a similar situation?

As our society progresses, however, we learn to understand the problems within our societal structure and address them. And the thought that men should be invincible is one of those problems. Today, we have the knowledge and the technology to determine and analyze mental health issues. Scientists now know that mental health issues occur due to various external factors such as stress and internal factors such as a chemical imbalance within our brains. Mood issues, for example, are often not that you're just feeling sad and not something you can simply stop.

So, thanks to society changing, more and more men are learning to be conscious of their mental health. But there's still a long way to go, as it is only a fraction of the total population of men that have started taking mental health seriously.

We must stop thinking about mental health as something binary and instead think of it on a continuum, in the same way as we do for physical health. We think nothing of trying to improve our physical fitness or admitting that our physical health seems to have taken a slight dip. Once we start seeing our mental health in the same way, we are much more open to using tools and techniques to improve it, and the stigma of working to improve our mental health gradually dissolves.

Prioritizing to Include You

The majority of us agree that taking care of our mental health should be a top priority. In theory, we understand the significance, but in practice, we often forget. For example, deadlines constantly dominate schedules, and our busy lives get in the way. Or we've just had too much to drink and sleep on it. Or the endless scrolling of our screens consumes us. Although we are now living in an "Age of Anxiety" and "global mental health crisis," many of us still have trouble prioritizing our mental health amid our never-ending to-do lists.

Next, the alarm clocks start ringing. According to the American Psychological Association, the first sign that you may be susceptible to stress or mental health problems may be a change in your physical health.

The World Health Organization predicts that by 2030, stress-related illnesses will become more common than infectious ones. Yet, at the same time, it is true that we are not powerless in the face of the stresses brought on by modern demands or the hardships that are a part of living.

Companies are trying to change course, while anxious staff and wary customers keep the public on edge. We worry about the security of those we care about. As committed fathers with young children, caring sons taking care of elderly parents, busy employees trying to build a successful career, or supportive friends and co-workers, we often find we shouldering a lot of responsibility.

It is essential to realize and remember that you are your most valuable asset through these times. Unfortunately, the vast majority of people ignore this reality. Before you can be present and do your best for your friends, family, and co-workers, you must be present for yourself. Put your energy into yourself and become the most valuable resource you can be, and you'll help everyone around you.

Focus on the mental aspects first

You should treat your mental health like any other investment. The account can only expand with regular deposits, and the interest rate can only be maintained through regular portfolio reviews.

Appreciating one another is crucial, so make an effort to interact with others in novel ways. Keep in touch with those closest to you, and keep up your meetings with people who make you feel positive. This might include your therapist or mentor or friends and family who you are comfortable and able to talk freely with.

Many people who are successful in life and business find regularly talking with a coach or mentor more helpful to their work and personal life than any other change they have made. High-flying executives often work with Executive Coaches, but they aren't just for Chief Executives. Anyone can benefit from having a structured conversation with a coach to help them work through their challenges and goals and develop a focused action plan to achieve them.

We must be careful not to keep relying on the routines and habits that have brought us solace even as the world around us spins out of control. Instead, make sure you give yourself time to think about where you are going and how you can improve things for yourself.

Do not forget your physical well-being.

Take the time to appreciate health for what it is and take deliberate, constructive steps to improve your physical health. For example, could you make more of an effort to eat healthily, get enough sleep, and, yes, make time for exercise?

In addition to the obvious physical benefits, regular exercise has a profound effect on your mental state, helping you to maintain a positive outlook and lessen the frequency and intensity of negative thoughts. Many people find that reserving the same time slot every day can make exercise a habit that they look forward to rather than dread.

When you prioritize your health, you improve your mental and physical performance and gain the stamina to carry through with challenging tasks like making essential decisions, implementing innovative business plans, and providing emotional and practical support to those who need you.

Let go of things that don't deserve your attention.

The fact that you are reading this book probably means that you are open to change – permit yourself to let go of the way things were. Many inherently dislike change, but it can be positive and rewarding when embraced. Remember to recognize any changes you make and be kind to yourself. Making change isn't easy, so pat yourself on the back as you reflect on the commitments you are making and the steps you are taking.

As you make changes to give yourself more time for self-care and improve your well-being, try to view this as a chance to start over in many areas and rid yourself of bad habits, toxic people in your life, and unhelpful professional aspirations. Create a plan to enhance your situation. Epictetus, a Greek philosopher, is credited with the adage, "It's not what happens to you; it's how you respond to it." Consider the present moment a window of opportunity to pour more resources into your goals and cast aside the nagging doubts and fears that have kept you from moving forward.

Spend more time and energy becoming the person you want to be and less time and effort becoming the person you believed you had to be. Spend some time improving yourself so you can be as effective as possible, not only for yourself but those around you.

How to Find That Work-Life Balance

Establishing a positive work-life balance is key to maintaining good mental health for any adult. Unfortunately, there probably isn't a single profession that doesn't come with its own stress. Whether you're a teacher, a plumber, a scientist, or anything else for that matter, your job is probably a primary source of stress.

In our society, we work to get paid for our contribution to meet our survival requirements. But when you take it too far, it can be pretty detrimental to your mental health.

Think for a minute - do you want to be rich and unhealthy, or healthy and poor? I bet neither. That's why it's all about finding that perfect balance between the two!

So, what do you do to find that balance?

Well, there are quite a few things that you can do to find the right balance, but the important thing is to understand how to separate your personal life from your professional life.

Leave your work at your workplace.

So many of us are guilty of bringing our work into our home life. Sometimes, it's just a simple task that has been delayed, so you do it at home. Sometimes, it's a crunch, and work is getting piled up faster than you can finish it. But, whatever the reason be, we've all done it. And unfortunately, for many, there's no way to escape work responsibilities completely, even at home.

But, leaving aside the times when you absolutely need to let work encroach on your home life, you should aim to avoid it. Stop letting work take up your non-work time unless you have no option, and be very strict with yourself on this.

Bringing your work into your home life not only takes away your valuable rejuvenation time but can also negatively affect your household relationships and your state of mind. So, treasure your own time – it is precious and don't give it up to work readily. Moreover, once people at your work realize that you have extra capacity and are willing to work in your own time, they'll be more open to contacting you regarding work-related things even when you're home. So, make a simple and strict policy to not bring work back to your home.

Establish social boundaries

Social boundaries in a workplace are essential. They dictate your relationship with your co-workers and how close you feel with your colleagues. Boundaries are important because your workplace is a professional space that has its own rules and regulations.

Making friends with your colleagues is okay, but always understand that your workplace is not somewhere you should be "too friendly" with others. Be mindful of what you say in front of others and pay attention to how other people treat you.

Learn to respect the rules of your workplace and set your boundaries accordingly so that you don't have to deal with unnecessary problems later on. There are many instances of people getting fired over the silliest jokes, the most casual remarks, and even something as simple as helping others out too much. You will probably find that you get more respect from colleagues with this approach too.

Having a clear boundary in your mind and differentiating the way you behave at work, compared to with friends and family, will lead to appropriate interactions and less work-related stress.

Learn to say 'no.'

Something that I've seen a lot of people struggle to do at work is say 'no'. Taking on more and more can lead to loss of job satisfaction and will significantly increase your stress levels. That said, it's not healthy to make rude rejections either. So here are some tips for saying 'no' to your boss and peers at work without making enemies.

Firstly, don't simply say 'no'; explain your thinking – for example, "No, I can't do an extra shift tonight - I'm keen to keep a positive work-life balance so that I can give more when I'm at work and keep healthy, but thank you for offering it to me".

When you say 'no', say it with confidence – look at the person you're talking to, and say it calmly, making sure there is no hesitation in your voice. You should be firm but not overstated.

Don't feel the need to make excuses or explain in detail – for example, if your boss asks you to do overtime, it's okay to say that you'd prefer to keep your non-work time. You don't need to describe what you're doing or explain that you've made commitments.

If, on the other hand, it's a peer asking for your time during the working day, you can make it clear that you are busy with work that your boss needs. For example - "I'm afraid I'm not going to be able to help with that – I've been asked to focus on an important piece of project work."

If your boss is asking you to do additional work, and you feel you already have enough to do, the easiest thing is to simply explain your priorities and the impact of taking on the extra work. You can do this in different ways, but one approach that many people find effective is to make the conversation about what your boss would like you to prioritize. That way, you can be willing and enthusiastic about the new work but clear that it won't all happen simultaneously. For example. "Of course, I can work on the new project – I have three pieces of work filling my time at the moment, so if we can have a conversation about priorities, I'll know where to focus and what order to do things."

Use a separate contact line for work.

Something that some people find extremely helpful is using a different contact number for work. It's such an effective way to separate work from personal life; it's a surprise that more people do not use this method.

Many smartphones nowadays support two SIMs, which means you can use two contact lines with the same phone. So, it's not difficult to maintain a separate line for work purposes.

Having a separate contact line makes it easier to distinguish when you're getting a call from your colleagues or boss. It also makes it easier to cut off contact so that you can enjoy your vacation peacefully without everyone calling you at random times. It's not an absolute necessity, but it's something to consider depending on the nature of your role.

Do not overwork yourself.

According to a study conducted by the World Health Organization (WHO) in 2016, around 488 million people were working long hours around the world. Since then, the number has only been increasing. This is concerning because the same study concluded that more than 745,000 people died that year from stroke and heart disease due to the stress of overworking. In addition, overworking can cause issues such as sleep deprivation, mood swings and a general lack of energy and make you unhappy.

However, the reality is harsh, and it can be difficult to avoid overworking even if you want to. This is even more true if you aren't yet as financially established or if you handle huge responsibilities at the workplace.

If you find yourself in such a situation, spend some time working out what you can delegate up, down, and to peers; what can wait; and what is draining your time unnecessarily and can stop – are there any meetings, for example, that you can skip, or low-value tasks that can wait.

When you find that you are very busy, one of the best ways to deal with it is to take a break at regular intervals to avoid building up too much stress. For example, try to get away from the workplace at lunchtime and take a walk – even 15 minutes can make a big difference to your state of mind.

You can also consider coaching to help you to work through your approach to work and identify and address the things that cause you stress. Many successful executives in large organizations believe coaching is essential in maintaining their focus and high pace without undue stress.

Taking a regular vacation, even just a long weekend, from time to time can do wonders for your mental health and energy levels.

Imperfection is okay

An issue that is more common amongst young workers who are just starting in a field is the problem of perfection. Younger minds are often inherently more passionate about their work and can be inclined to put in much more effort than others in the workplace. Thus, it is understandable that many chase perfection in their work.

That, however, can translate to problems later on. In a professional environment, that can be disastrous for several reasons. Firstly, in such environments, a chain through which work progresses often exists. Someone spending too much time trying to make everything perfect will eventually drag down the whole process and make it slower.

But while this affects the workplace, it also affects the individuals because achieving perfection is a difficult task that can suck up a person's time and effort. Moreover, it can be incredibly demotivating and stressful when you still do not reach the "perfection" that you desire after spending so much of your time and effort. Therefore, finding the perfect balance of imperfection in your work can be beneficial not only for you but also for your employer!

Remember the 80-20 rule: 20% of the effort generate 80% of the output, usually the first 80%. Ask yourself if that is good enough. And if not, at least be conscious that your increasing time investment is bringing diminishing returns.

Don't let the great be the enemy of the good!

Learning to use a team effectively

There's a reason why most big companies dedicate entire teams to even the smallest tasks. It is no secret that when humans work together, we can achieve things that are quite literally impossible for individuals. So, teamwork can be essential in many situations.

However, the most important thing a team allows is the ability to divide work. Writing a detailed report of 100 pages within a day might be difficult for one person, but with the help of a few more people, it can suddenly feel like a trivial task. If you have a job where you are part of a team, make sure that you let everyone do their jobs so that you can focus on your own. Relying on your team doesn't mean that you let your team do everything for you. It just means that you trust them to do what they do best so that you can focus on doing what you do best.

Starting New Hobbies

Relaxation and enjoyment are an absolute necessity when it comes to managing your mental and physical health. Working throughout the whole day is not only going to get boring, but it's also unhealthy. But what do you do when you have time on your hand and are not working?

Sitting idly around is one option for relaxation, but that is only good for a little while. You'll soon either get bored or get too lazy to return to work.

Hobbies are a great way to keep yourself engaged during such times while also enjoying what you are doing. Not everyone has jobs that they can genuinely enjoy, but hobbies – they are for everyone!

We all have different things that interest us, and what we consider a hobby depends on us. For example, some of us are more interested in sports, some like reading, some play video games, and so on.

Hobbies are fun, but they also contribute to our well-being. In addition, they are unique in the sense that they can be a great way to regulate stress while being productive at the same time.

For example, if you play sports, you're working your physical body out and reducing stress levels. If you like reading, you are learning whilst you recharge your batteries. No matter your hobby, it probably has several other benefits. Maybe it is an excellent way to vent out pent-up energy from working long hours or shouldering too many responsibilities.

However, sometimes it can be challenging to find a new hobby that you enjoy, especially if you don't know where to start. Even if you already have hobbies that you enjoy, it's always good to start exploring new things.

Here are some suggestions for finding a new hobby.

Try different things before settling for one.

There are quite literally thousands of activities that can qualify as a hobby for you. If you enjoy doing something that provides a productive value to you, it doesn't matter what the activity is; you can probably turn it into a hobby. So, for example, if you enjoy tinkering with your car, listening to music, or spending time in the garden, these things can form the basis of perfect hobbies.

When choosing a new hobby, the trick is to try out a lot of things before you settle on one that you know for sure is for you. For many of us, there are certain things that we find ourselves interested in at the beginning. We are initially very engaged, but as we start immersing ourselves in the activity, we realize that the interest is fleeting.

Get your feet wet in as many activities as you can. Consider your options, and evaluate how they can help you and how they make you feel. When you engage in many activities, you'll find it easier to understand which ones you enjoy and want to continue rather than simply admire the people involved with them from a distance.

Bring out your inner child.

Here's another piece of advice: bring your inner child to make the decision for you. Not sure what I mean? I'll explain.

As children, our intentions and interests are pure and simple. We enjoy doing things that we find fun. Nothing else matters too much at that moment. So we just engage ourselves in what we are doing wholeheartedly.

As we grow up, we start getting better at suppressing those feelings. To a great extent, our society decides what we should enjoy doing and what not. We adjust our tastes and preferences to match those around us, consciously or subconsciously. Hence, letting go of these restrictions and bringing out your inner child can be a great way to make sure that you're honest to yourself about what you enjoy doing and what you don't.

As a child, we have so many things we do simply for the fun of it. We play games, watch cartoons, and even invent new ways to have fun. When it comes to choosing a hobby for yourself, letting that child do the deciding rather than your adult self can be a great way to make sure that you will enjoy whatever it is that you settle on.

Let your creativity guide you.

Many people might argue that creativity is something you either have or don't, but that's simply not true. We are all inherently creative and have creative skills that we either put to good use in what we do or keep suppressed because that's not something our job requires.

That said, your creativity can be an excellent asset when trying to find the perfect hobby. Creative hobbies are some of the best ones not only because they're fun and enjoyable but also because being creative is inherently productive.

Creative hobbies can be challenging to get into, especially since most people think you "either have the talent for it or don't". But again, that's quite far from the truth. People who are good at creative activities are so because they spend time being creative, work on their skills, and strive to improve. Like any other field where people work their way up through their effort, "creative people" are the same.

So, don't be afraid to explore your creative side and find something that interests you, even if you're not "good" at it right from the get-go. Pick up that guitar that's been gathering dust and play a few songs. Get yourself some brushes and colors and paint something. Take your old diary out and write a poem. When you let your creativity guide you, you also start getting more in touch with your emotions and feelings, which can in turn, help your mental health.

Reflect and pay attention to what you enjoy doing

What we enjoy doing doesn't have to be anything too complicated. Most of us probably have some such activities that aren't really what you'd call a hobby, but we enjoy doing them nevertheless. Sometimes the simplest things are the ones that bring us the most happiness. For example, I appreciate household chores such as cleaning or laundry. Such activities do not require too much brainpower but are also essential and contribute to your productivity. Blast some of your favourite music on the speakers, and you might enjoy the most trivial chores.

These activities can be quite a healthy replacement for your usual hobbies, so don't be afraid to enjoy your time with them. Keep a lookout for the type of everyday activities that you enjoy, and then reflect on why you like doing them. Doing so will give you an idea of what you want to look for in activities you do for fun. Going back to my example, the reason I love doing such activities is probably because I can keep myself busy while also listening to some good music, all while letting my mind relax, reducing any mental and physical stress.

Making Time for You

Making it happen

When we talk about self-care, we're talking about the little things you do regularly to look after and improve your physical and mental well-being. You may have heard about self-care and are on board with its benefits, even if it requires additional effort, or it may be a new concept for you.

Taking care of yourself entails paying attention to your body, checking in with yourself regularly, and questioning your habits and beliefs when you notice something isn't quite right in your life. Getting started can be a challenge. The first step toward self-care is to let go of the notion that there is a "perfect" or "right" method to go about it. Of course, your self-care doesn't have to be confined to soaking in a photo-worthy bath on Instagram. (Though if you love a good bubble bath, go for it!) From getting more sleep to spending time with the right people, I'll share some practical self-care tips with you.

Firstly, make it a priority to incorporate self-care into your life. Some of your self-care routines can be included daily, others weekly or monthly – the critical thing is to make sure you make time for yourself regularly. Most of us understand the need for self-care but have difficulty putting it into regular practice, so you need to focus on making this happen. When you're trying to balance multiple demands on your time, it's easy to neglect your personal needs. Your occasional social trips, salon appointments, and gym sessions may qualify as self-care. Still, it's really the regular activities that refresh you and make you feel good that are the true definition of self-care. If you don't take time for self-care regularly, you're more likely to experience feelings of stress and exhaustion. Taking care of your mind, body, and soul is essential to being the best version of yourself. Self-care gives you the energy to show up as your best self in the world around you every day.

The types of behaviors that you consider to be self-care are dependent on your point of view. Say, for example, that you're new to jogging and your weekly mileage goal is 10 kilometers. When you first begin jogging, you may find that the activity is not fun, and you may struggle through each step of the process. However, it may still be rewarding if you enjoy the sense of accomplishment that comes from achieving your goals. Even if it doesn't feel like self-care at the time, when you can look back and say, "Look at what I did today," that counts, and you've succeeded in making progress towards your objective.

Here are some recommendations to help you include self-care into your daily routine and stick to it.

Planning and scheduling

A lack of *planning* your self-care will likely lead to a lack of *achieving* self-care. So, make time for self-care a non-negotiable commitment. Make a note of it in your calendar and, if necessary, send yourself a reminder. For example, set aside 30 minutes in the morning and 30 minutes at night to read or practice yoga or another self-care activity of your choice. Share the times you'll be unavailable with your family or housemates. Make it as official as you can get it. Having a strategy and scheduling self-care in your daily calendar makes it easier to fit in and protect the time.

Something as simple as laying out your clothing, or getting your bag ready, or preparing food for the next day the night before is a type of self-care. In giving yourself some time to get things ready at a leisurely pace you might help ease some of the morning tension.

Be open to new possibilities

Your self-care regimen should be flexible enough that you can experiment with different ways of executing it. There are days when self-care will be a breeze and others when it will seem impossible. Things will inevitably get in the way. When this occurs, it's critical to let go of control a little. Every day is a new opportunity to get back on track, so don't be too hard on yourself.

There will be flaws in your self-care regimen. Make it a point to experiment with self-care goals; try to include activities that involve moving your body regularly, along with activities that nourish your mind. Establish a foundation whilst also being open to new ideas and approaches.

Breathe in the correct aromas

Breathing exercises have been shown to help us relax. As crucial as *how* we breathe is *what* we breathe. Scientists are still debating the benefits of aromatherapy. But studies have shown that citrus fragrances, especially orange essential oil, reduce tension and anxiety when life hands you lemons! And some people's memory may be improved by inhaling the scent of rosemary. Finding relaxing scents is immensely individual; what one person finds relaxing, another finds irritating. Try using candles, infusers, or bottles of essential oils to diffuse your favorite aromas and help create an atmosphere that matches your needs and soothes your mind.

The Apparent Charm

The days when a man's hygiene routine consisted of nothing more than a bar of musk-infused soap and some spicy aftershaves are over. These days, both men and women tend to make time for regular skincare.

As a man in today's society, there is always pressure to look your best - whether in the boardroom or at a weekend festival. Because of this, caring for one's skin has become an essential component of many men's routines.

There are some physiological distinctions between male and female skin. Because of the more significant influence of male hormones, men have more, larger sebaceous glands, which produce oil. This means that men's skin tends to be oilier and thicker. Because of their oilier skin, men tend to need to wash their faces frequently. However, if the wrong product is used, the skin's natural moisture can be entirely stripped away by this process.

Regular cleanser, moisturizer, and sunscreen will help your skin feel and look better for years to come. A few minutes a day to preserve your youthful appearance is as simple as sticking to a regular skincare program. Many cosmetic companies target women and emphasize skin care as part of a woman's daily beauty routine. But guys, skin care isn't just something women should worry about; you should, too. Taking care of your skin does not have to be complicated or need a wide range of products. Instead, it should be a regular habit, like cleaning your teeth.

But why do I need it?

A registered professional psychotherapist and a psychodermatologist in Santa Barbara, California, Matt Traube emphasizes the importance of maintaining healthy habits such as eating well, exercising regularly, keeping a journal, and taking care of one's skin. He explains that those habits are essential for maintaining physical and mental well-being.

A study published in June 2018 in the Lancet Psychiatry indicated that major depressive disorder, bipolar disorder, mood issues, loneliness, and lower happiness were more common in those who lacked consistent routines throughout the active sections of their day.

These Selfcare habits make you feel good and give you a sense of security. You anchor your day and give you a sense of regularity throughout the week. You could even feel a sense of minor achievement.

Many patients with anxiety and depression say their symptoms worsen in the 30 minutes to an hour before bedtime. According to Traube, many people experience increased stress during this period because they have more free time. Taking care of your face by washing, toning, and moisturizing is a great way to clear your mind and concentrate on the task. (This is true of anything that keeps you occupied, whether it's a new project, making dinner, or walking the dog around the block.)

Caring for one's skin is another way to practice mindfulness. Practicing mindfulness, as discussed earlier, entails paying attention to your internal and external feelings in the here-and-now without evaluating them — the soothing feel of warm water as you wash your face, for instance.

More than 1,100 adults who participated in March 2019 in Frontiers in Psychology found that this simple exercise alone reduced their levels of melancholy and anxiety by preventing them from dwelling on negative thoughts. By engaging in this simple practice, you can keep yourself looking younger as you age and help your brain disconnect from less healthy, spiraling thinking processes in just a few minutes.

Limit social media and screen time

Social media has helped spread positivity and joy, but it can also seriously impact mental health. Social media is a quick way to connect with friends and family, but it also has the potential to take away your ability to disconnect. It's no secret that social media can negatively affect your mind. The constant checking and refreshing of social media can lead to anxiety or depression.

Though the effects of social media on our psych are multifaceted, they're often a reflection of the underlying factors that might be changing our personality and outlook as it does. For example, many people experience anxiety, sleepless nights, or other symptoms from interacting with their followers. However, what is less acknowledged, is that social media can also directly alter your personality and life outlook.

Here are some ways that social media can affect your mental health:

It's addictive.

Many people spend hours scrolling through their feeds, liking or commenting on posts, and sharing updates with their friends. Unfortunately, this makes it difficult for them to focus on other tasks, such as work, because they're constantly distracted by their phones.

It's isolating.

Social media allows people to stay connected with others without having face-to-face interactions. The problem is that reading posts, especially from someone you don't know in real life, doesn't feel as personal or meaningful as when you're talking with someone face-to-face."

It can make us feel bad about ourselves.

A recent study found that people who spend more time on social media spend less time working out or doing other activities that require physical movement or exercise. Another study found that people who spend more than four hours per day on Facebook tend not to get sufficient sleep, leading to increased stress levels and even depression symptoms such as irritability and anxiety.

It can increase stress.

Social media can also negatively affect our brains by increasing stress levels and causing us to become less present in real-life situations. According to an article from Psychology Today, "People who use social networking sites are more likely to experience higher levels of stress than non-users."

Even when you're not using social media, staying on your phone, or any other screen for that matter, for too long isn't good for you. It can be challenging to resist the pull of our phones and other devices, but too much screen time has many long-term and short-term adverse effects. Physical strain in the eyes is one of the most common among them. Others include sleep deprivation and reduced cognitive ability. Not to mention that you are also probably wasting a lot of time that could be put to better use!

So, what can you do? Try these tips:

Have a set time each day when you don't check your phone or any other device — maybe an hour before dinner or after lunch. That way, you have time to relax without being tempted by your phone!

Alternatively, turn that on its head, and try to use your phone *only* at set times each day, so that you can focus on other tasks when they come up instead of just zoning out while looking at your screen.

Go out for vacations and getaways. Explore new territories, especially places where you probably won't get any cellphone reception. Try to spend a few days avoiding screen time as much as possible and see how that feels – is it freeing?

How Can Mindfulness Help?

Become aware of your thoughts and feelings.

It's possible to experience freedom and health in the present moment using an approach called mindfulness, which is becoming increasingly popular in psychotherapy. Mindfulness, a Buddhist idea, is a meditation technique that teaches you to pay attention to and be at peace with your feelings and bodily sensations. According to research, being in touch with yourself through mindfulness enhances your mental health and reduces stress. We also gain a more accurate picture of ourselves when we practice mindfulness.

The mindful approach

The mindful approach involves focusing your mind on the here and now and being relaxed. You can do this by making sure you have 10 minutes or more when you won't be disturbed.

Sit in a comfortable position and relax. Take a few slow deep breaths. As you exhale, consciously let the tension release from your body. Exhale and relax your shoulders, exhale and relax your back, then your legs, arms, and face in turn. Then allow your breathing to become normal, and focus on your breathing. Notice the rise and fall of your tummy and chest as you breathe.

Now let your thoughts drift away, and when you notice your mind has started thinking about something, calmly acknowledge that and bring your focus back to your breathing.

Another way to use mindfulness is to bring it into your daily activities. We do so much on autopilot these days, and we multitask where we can rather than focusing. The technique here is for whilst doing an everyday activity, such as walking to work or making dinner. Rather than let your subconscious mind take over, and your conscious mind wander, you focus your full attention and all your senses on what you are doing.

For example, next time you walk to work, think about the temperature of the air and how the breeze feels on your skin. Notice whether you feel hot or cool – do different parts of your body feel differently? Observe the sounds around you – can you hear traffic? Can you hear anything over the traffic? How do the traffic sounds change as you walk? Do you make any noise as you walk? What scents can you detect? Do they remind you of anything? Are they pleasant or unpleasant? Do they gradually get stronger or fade away?

By focusing your full attention and observing what all your senses tell you, in the here and now, you will gain a whole new appreciation for the world around you, and your mind can be calm and relaxed.

This mindfulness technique takes time and practice, but you can build it into your everyday activities, and it's incredible how much better ten minutes of mindfulness can make you feel.

Try mindful eating

Studies have shown that mindful eating can help you to control your eating patterns, lose weight, curb your appetite, and improve your mood. It is by professionals to treat eating disorders, depression, anxiety, and a variety of food-related illnesses. It works by helping you to achieve a state of full attention to your eating experiences, urges, and physical cues.

Mindful eating entails:

- Reducing the amount of time spent eating.
- Eating only until you are physically satisfied.
- Using your five senses to take in the sights, sounds, scents, textures, and tastes around you.
- Observing how eating affects your mood and your physical appearance.
- Appreciating the taste and quality of your meals.

It can help you to

- Distinguish between hunger and non-hunger-related food cravings.
- Develop coping mechanisms for food-related guilt and anxiety
- Maintain a healthy diet for general well-being.

All of this allows you to take control of your automatic responses and ideas and replace them with more healthy ones.

Is Mindful eating worth a try?

Food options are many in today's fast-paced culture. Distractions, such as televisions, laptops, and cellphones, have redirected our attention away from the actual act of eating. Mindless eating has become the norm, with most meals consumed in minutes.

Unfortunately, your brain can take up to 20 minutes to register that you're full. This means that if you eat too quickly, the fullness signal may not arrive until you've already overeaten. Unfortunately, as a result of binge eating, this is quite prevalent.

Mindful eating helps you regain focus and calm down, making eating an act of choice rather than a reflexive one. More than that, you'll learn how to tell the difference between emotional and physical hunger by strengthening your ability to recognize physical hunger and fullness indicators. Increased self-awareness can help you avoid overeating in the absence of hunger. When you're aware of your triggers, you can put some distance between yourself and your reaction, allowing you more control over how you respond.

We all know that most diets don't work in the long run, which is no secret. Most obese people who lose weight return to their pre-diet weight within a few years following their weight loss. Overeating in reaction to hunger pangs and emotional eating leads to weight gain and the regaining of lost pounds. Chronic stress may also significantly influence the development of obesity and overeating. Research shows you can reduce weight by modifying your eating habits and reducing stress. Participants in a 6-week group seminar on mindful eating lost an average of 9 pounds (4 kilograms) each. In the six-month follow-up period, ongoing weight loss was an average of 26 pounds (12 kg), with no weight regain in the subsequent three months. Participants reported that awareness and increased self-control replaced the bad sensations linked with eating and generally felt happier as they changed their thinking about food. The evidence suggests that you have a much better chance of long-term weight loss success if you address your unhealthy eating habits.

The Practice

Many of us can't eat as consciously as people can do on retreat or during mindfulness training, especially with families, careers, and the countless distractions around us. Our loved ones and co-workers may not be willing to sit down and eat with us if we take a long time to eat each bite. One approach is to eat some meals mindfully, slowly savouring every bite, where opportunity permits. Although this is a slower approach, it is much more practical for busy people and still brings benefits, just on a longer timeframe. If you are lucky enough to have more time to explore mindful eating, you could also seek out more formal opportunities, such as mindfulness eating retreats.

Wait for your body to catch up.

The body transmits a satiation signal around 20 minutes after eating enough, which makes it very easy to overindulge. Eating too quickly exacerbates this, and if you ignore your body's cues, you overeat and gain weight. Slowing down allows your body and brain to catch up, allowing you to receive your body's messages about how much to consume. Many of your grandmother's habits, such as sitting down to eat, chewing each bite 25 times (or more), placing your fork down between meals, and other seemingly unnecessary etiquette, can be simple ways to slow down. Simply eating more slowly and paying more attention to the signs your body sends you can be beneficial.

Be aware of your unique hunger cues.

As with many mindfulness techniques, we may gain greater insight by first focusing on our bodies rather than our intellect. We may learn to listen to our bodies instead of just eating when we feel stressed, upset, frustrated, lonely, or bored, which may be different for everyone. Feeling low on energy or a little dizzy? You may be suffering from a food craving. Often we eat when our minds tell us to, rather than when our bodies tell us to. To eat mindfully, we must pay close attention to our body's cues that tell us when we're hungry. How do you know when you're physically hungry? And how do you know when you're emotionally hungry?

Bring mindfulness to the kitchen.

One of the ways we eat mindlessly is by strolling around, looking through cabinets, and eating at odd times and places rather than thinking proactively about our meals and snacks. Doing this makes us less likely to form healthy eating habits and less susceptible to external cues telling us what and how much to eat. Of course, snacking is normal, but eating at regular intervals can improve your mental and physical well-being and your mood and sleep routine.

To achieve this, we must sit down, put our meal on a plate or dish, and use utensils rather than our hands. Eating together is also beneficial because you get a good connection, calm down, and enjoy the food and conversation even more. In addition, we tend to follow our dinner partner's lead and so are less likely to over or undereat because of our emotions.

Make sure your kitchen is organized to support healthy eating and nourish social interactions. In the kitchen, think about how and where you store things. Are nutritious foods readily available? Do you see any food in the immediate area? We eat when there is food available.

Of course, your eating habits may change during different seasons or on special occasions, so don't stress about it. Feeling guilty about this can lead to overindulging, so be kind to yourself and allow yourself some flexibility for special occasions.

It's generally not a good idea to do grocery shopping if you're hungry, but there's a medium ground. Customers who buy greens are more likely to head to the ice cream or alcohol sections than those who do not, according to a psychological effect known as "moral licensing." We believe our karma will eventually "even out," and we can use it to indulge in junk food or engage in other less-than-desirable actions. Just being aware and conscious of this can help you to avoid it.

Conscious lifestyle

Increasing your self-awareness can boost your performance in all areas of your life. Conscious living is about taking charge of your life, rather than making decisions without thinking. Rather than accepting the energy that comes our way, it's time to take back control. If you're feeling lost or unsure of where you're going, it's possible that living more consciously will be your most significant life decision ever.

Changing too many things overnight, though, isn't usually the best strategy - decide where to focus and bring in changes gradually. Conscious living is a way of life, a skill, and an art form. It's not something you do once and then forget about, it requires an ongoing change, but it is something you can do every day of your life and not feel guilty about.

Consciously and thoughtfully, doing everything you do is surprisingly simple. Try taking the time to think about what you're doing before you do it. While it may seem evident at first, it's astonishing how few people do this and how easy it is to live life on autopilot and repeat the routines we've always done. It's challenging to change our lives and break out of our habits, but once you start living more consciously, it's amazing how enjoyable everyday tasks can be!

Try factoring in some of these more mindful techniques too

Make retrospective thinking part of your daily habit: No matter how you choose to do it — whether you keep a journal, incorporate reflection into your evening routine, schedule a weekly session to assess your life, or take some time away from the workplace to think about everything — you should do so regularly. By doing this, you will find that you start to focus on the things that are more important to you.

Set or reassess your life's goals at least once a year: What are your long-term goals? What matters most to you? What kind of life do you wish to lead? Can you get there? Write it down and store it where you'll see it frequently. As a result, you begin moving more purposefully towards your goals and feeling more content and satisfied.

Examine your relationships: The people we care about are often the most significant aspect of our lives. Consider your interpersonal connections. How much time do you spend with people? Do you show your gratitude to the people around you as much as you would like? Do any of your relationships have room for improvement? If so, are there any obstacles that can be overcome? Is there any way to improve communication? Reevaluate your working relationships as well. Humans are social creatures, and we should not underestimate the positive impact that fulfilling relationships can have on our mental and physical health.

Take a moment to reflect on your impact on the world: What impact are your actions having on the environment and on others? Whether you think about it or not, your actions have consequences. Knowing your impact on others can help you to feel connected and valued in the world. For example, a simple thing like making sure you recycle where possible can make you feel optimistic about playing your role in helping the planet and being part of a community.

Take into account the actual cost of each item: Often, we don't stop to consider the actual price of the items we purchase. "It was only $10, so there's no problem." However, you cannot recover the time spent earning those 10 dollars. Consider what kind of life you want – are you comfortable working as much as you do so that your hard-earned money can go on more frivolous expenses? There is some merit in the saying, "Take care of the pennies, and the dollars will take care of themselves"

Things in your life may not be as cheap as you think: Our homes and workplaces are often crammed with *things.* This is not only a financial burden; it's also a mental and emotional one. The more items we have, the more we need to organize and clean and the less space we have in our homes. Sometimes we have difficulty finding things that we know we have as a result. Visual stress can be caused by 'things' taking up space in our daily lives. Those who are dedicated to a minimalist lifestyle swear by it, and find it makes them more relaxed and content. Of course, being minimalistic isn't for everyone, but there is a halfway house. Even just reducing the clutter in a few cupboards or draws at a time or in a single room can begin to bring you feelings of positivity. Start small, and let your de-cluttering grow!

Analyze your daily routine to see where you can make improvements: Conduct a time audit and keep a diary of how exactly you spend your time for at least a week. When you audit your time, the results can be shocking! People often feel like they are wasting time doing things that aren't how they want to spend their lives, and this is the point! Knowing how you spend your time gives you the knowledge you need to make better choices about how you spend your time in the future. Once you can see where your time goes, find the things that aren't bringing you happiness and plan how to reduce or eliminate your time spent on them.

Be clear about who you are: Think about who you are, your principles, what you stand for, and what you hold dear in life. What do you want people to say about your life and legacy when you are no longer with us?

As an exercise, write down:

- your top 3 values;
- 3 things you'd like to do more of and
- 3 things you'd like to do less of.

Just doing this exercise helps focus the mind and will give you the impetus to make positive changes in your life. See if you can find a way to make an instant change to enable you to do more of what you desire now…today!

Take a look at how you respond to the little things in life. Are you sometimes guilty of avoidance, denial, rationalization, procrastination, or blaming others? Do you need to take more responsibility for any of your actions; or seek help or guidance? Stand back, become objective, look at the areas where you're weaker, and then brainstorm new ways to deal with them by writing down whatever comes to mind initially. You can later refine your brainstorm notes by picking out one or two things to do.

Consider what matters to you the most. We all have different desires and motivations for our lives, whether wanting a better relationship with our loved ones or hoping to be a better person. There are many reasons why we wish for these things. The secret to success is finding your true self and connecting with it. Deep fulfilment comes from within, not from external stimuli or fleeting aspirations.

To better understand yourself, write down the traits of your fundamental self that you wish to tap into: for example, compassion, strength, truthfulness, power, focused attention, knowledge, and so on. Then, considering this list, note the key things you want to accomplish in life – you can include your professional life too, but make the focus your personal life. Finally, pick out your top five priorities from this list, and use them from now on, to guide what you do and where you focus your efforts and your precious time.

Health the Holistic Way

The idea that being healthy means "not becoming sick" has permeated our minds since childhood. These days a lot more goes into healthcare than we previously imagined. However, despite all that Western medicine has accomplished to make the world a safer place, many of us still have reservations about the field.

To augment what western medicine often lacks in terms of instruction on how to live an optimally healthy and vibrant life, the holistic approach to health and well-being seeks to fill that void.

Is the first thing that comes to mind when someone mentions "holistic health" some form of complementary or alternative medicine? If that's the case, you're somewhat correct. In addition, holistic health incorporates complementary therapies that have been scientifically proven to be effective. Like alternative medicine, it focuses on wellness and prevention rather than merely treating disease symptoms. However, integrating Eastern and Western medicine is only one aspect of holistic therapy. It's a broader, more individualized approach to well-being that considers everything about you. Taking care of your physical, mental, spiritual, and social well-being are all aspects of holistic health.

There have been cases where people have refused to take medicine because of their spiritual views and ended up getting sick or dying. However, it is entirely appropriate for a holistically healthy person to see a doctor and use western medicine. They may also want to complement that approach with changes to their diet or exercise regime, yoga, massage, acupuncture or some of the self-care techniques we've already covered for a whole body and mind approach to health.

Because your health is intertwined, a lack of strength in one area will impact your whole well-being. As an example, think about stress. Some physical symptoms, such as headaches and difficulty sleeping, can also be caused by this psychological response. Of course, the inverse is also true, and being ill can make you anxious or depressed. Spirituality and close relationships, on the other hand, can improve your physical and mental well-being. You can lower your blood pressure and stress levels by forming close friendships. You can also increase your chances of surviving cancer. This is why doctors who follow a more comprehensive approach to patient care don't just focus on your symptoms; they inquire about your overall health and lifestyle so that they can tailor their advice to your specific needs.

Taking a Look Outside the Box

Holistic health care providers use a variety of clinically established therapies to address a wide range of wellness concerns, from surgery and medications to dietary adjustments and exercise regimens, as well as psychological and spiritual counseling. Acupuncture, massage, or yoga may be recommended as complementary therapies for those who can benefit. Holistic healthcare providers may prescribe medicine or recommend surgery to treat an injury, but, for example, they may also recommend that you improve your endorphin levels naturally by exercising more. They'll inquire about your diet and explain how particular foods can cause inflammation and others can reduce it. They will ask about your level of stress (as well as your level of anxiety and depression). Therapies such as acupuncture for nerve pain, massage to relax muscles, and mindfulness meditation for stress and pain management are all options that your holistic doctor may suggest. They're not going to treat the symptom; they're going to treat the person, and they're going to use every instrument they have.

Access to Health Care

Being healthy is an important aim that is not always easy to achieve. It involves you making choices about what you eat and drink, levels of exercise, how much sleep you get, abstaining from certain vices, and making more time for yourself. Self-care can be challenging to fit into the craziness of work and life, making it more difficult to focus on your own needs.

A holistic doctor teaches you how to make better decisions and inspires you to do so. To avoid overwhelming you with a long list of lifestyle adjustments, they work with you to prioritize and help you select the changes that will impact your health the most to start first.

To achieve your wellness objectives, they work with you to develop a unique strategy for your needs and connect you with appropriate resources. Treating the whole person with various scientifically proven therapies recognizes the mind-body connection. An essential part of being healthy is building a solid relationship with a doctor who cares about your well-being and takes a holistic approach.

Physical Activity

One of the most cost-effective ways to enhance your general health is to engage in regular physical activity. Exercise has numerous health benefits, including lowering your risk of heart disease, stroke, type 2 diabetes, and some malignancies. In addition, working out has been demonstrated to improve sleep quality, raise self-esteem and lift your spirits, and reduce the risk of developing stress-related illnesses, including depression, Alzheimer's, and dementia.

A minimum of 150 minutes of physical activity each week is recommended for adults by the Department of Health and Human Services. Regular exercisers are said to have a more positive self-perception, better recall of events, and a more restful night's sleep. In addition, finding a physical activity you enjoy will help you stay motivated and consistent with your workouts. So, try different activities and approaches to find the right one for you. For example, watching your favourite TV show or listening to uplifting music while on the exercise bike might make the activity more pleasurable.

Taking care of one's entire self is what is meant by a holistic approach to life. Your health and well-being will improve as you take an integrated approach to your lifestyle.

Home Work Out

Many people find that, rather than spend their precious time going to and from the gym, they would rather exercise in the convenience and comfort of their own home. Some people spend the money they save on a gym membership on things such as an exercise bike, weights, a treadmill, or yoga equipment, but this isn't necessary. You can clear out a place in your living room and get ready to sweat.

Why at home?

In addition to saving money on gym membership and time travelling to the gym, there are many potential advantages to working out at home. For a start, it's much easier to fit a workout into a busy schedule, and we need to exercise more than ever when we're under the strain of dealing with a busy schedule!

The gym accentuates many people's insecurities. While working out at home, you don't have to worry about others noticing your clumsy attempts at a new activity, the insane amount of sweat you're generating (or the fact that you're not sweating), or your clothing and how you appear. Nothing will make you self-conscious like people who make working out look so very easy!

Not having to share equipment can be a real benefit too. There's nothing worse than going to the gym and seeing a puddle of sweat on your favorite piece of gym equipment from the prior user. And depending on your health situation, you may wish to avoid the germs and viruses you find in the shared commercial gym environment.

You can choose the music, TV show or podcast at home. Working out can be much more enjoyable when you can listen to whatever you want and at whatever volume. Forget about those irritating earbuds that keep falling out! Even singing out a few songs might help you tone your core. Make it a joyous occasion! Here are a few beginner sets for you:

Bridge

Make use of a bridge to work on stabilizing your core and strengthening your posterior chain. This is an excellent warm-up exercise.

- This exercise is best done on a flat surface with both knees bent and feet flat on the ground.
- Lift your bottom off the ground, clenching your glutes at the top as you push through your feet and brace your core.
- Repeat the movement while slowly returning to the beginning position.

Chair squat

Use the chair squat to strengthen your legs and core, make everyday activities easier, and improve posture.

- Set yourself up in front of the chair, feet shoulder-width apart and toes somewhat outward-pointing.
- Extend your arms out in front of you as you drop your back to the chair, hunched at your hips and bending your knees.
- Return to the starting position by pressing up through your heels.

Knee pushup

To build strength before trying a conventional pushup, try this beginner-style pushup.

- To begin, bend your knees and hold a high plank position.
- Lower yourself to the ground by bending your elbows while keeping your body straight from your head to your knees.
- Push up by straightening your arms again.

Stationary lunge

A stationary lunge works your quads, hamstrings, and glutes.

- Split your stance in front with your right leg. When you stand, your right foot should be flat on the ground, and your left foot should be on its toes.
- Bend your right knee and lunge until your right thigh is parallel to the ground.
- Return to the beginning position and repeat until you've done the required number of repetitions.
- Swap legs, and repeat the exercise on the other side.

Plank to Downward Dog

This maneuver will put your shoulders to the test. Shoulder exercises do not require the use of weights, after all.

- Assume a high plank stance with your feet and hands piled beneath your shoulders.
- Keep your core engaged while piking your hips up and back into the Downward Dog position. Your hands and feet should remain motionless. The body and ground should form a triangle. Keep your neck straight. Your eyes should be on your feet at all times.
- Return to the plank after a brief pause here. Repeat.

Straight-leg donkey kick

Donkey kicks are a great way to strengthen your glutes.

- Lie on your back with your legs bent and your hands directly under your shoulders.
- Aim towards the imaginary wall behind you while maintaining a straight leg and a straight back.
- Keep your foot flexed (toes pointed down to the floor). Be careful not to hunch your back or hunch your shoulders. At the apex, tighten your buttocks.
- Make your way back to the beginning. Repeat as many times as desired.

Bird Dog

The Bird Dog position is a full-body exercise. Despite its complexity, you can scale it depending on your ability. If you're a newbie, use this version.

- On all fours, place your hands and knees straight from your shoulders to your hips.
- Keep your hips square to the ground while simultaneously extending your left arm and right leg, and keep your neck neutral. This is when you should take two seconds to breathe.

- Turn around and head backward. Then switch to your right arm and left leg and do the same on the other side.

The gym

It's important you note that working out at home isn't the best option for everyone. Many people find that going out of the house or meeting a friend to exercise is more motivating, and if you are lucky enough to live or work near a good, affordable gym, that might be the best option for you.

Meditation and yoga

If you find it difficult to maintain a workout routine at home, meditation and yoga are two great alternatives to work on both your mental and physical health. Meditation especially is more suited for mental health benefits, while yoga can provide a good balance between both.

Meditation

Meditation, in short, is the activity of concentrating on something with the aim of reflecting on your thoughts and emotions. As a result, you become more aware of the environment and increase your mindfulness. There are several ways that people approach meditation, but it is undoubtedly a great way to spend some time with and learn more about yourself.

Meditation has several benefits.

It helps you control your negative emotions: Meditation is a very effective method for learning to control your emotions. Meditating even once every day can be a game changer for people who find it challenging to manage their anger or frustration.

It improves your imagination and creativity: Being in charge of your emotions and feelings means that you will be more imaginative and creative, which can be a great way to improve your creative capability.

It increases self-awareness: Part of the process of meditation is reflecting on yourself, and this includes everything about you, including your strengths, weaknesses, biases, skills, behavior, and so on. As you self-reflect, you naturally gain self-awareness, which can be incredibly helpful in many aspects of your life.

It helps manage stress and anxiety: One of the most incredible things about meditation is that it helps you calm your mind and soul. As a result, it is one of the best methods for managing stress levels and issues such as anxiety and depression.

It has several physical health benefits: In addition to having mental health benefits and helping you grow as a person, meditation has several health benefits for your physical body. For example, it is known that meditation helps reduce blood pressure, regulate mood swings, and even improve your memory. In addition, it can also help improve your pain tolerance and be incredibly effective in battling addiction issues.

Yoga

Originating in ancient India and having been practiced since around 500-200 BC, Yoga is an activity that has an incredible and remarkable effect on our body, mind, and soul. It was initially viewed as a way of life that brings harmony to these three elements, thus keeping a person "healthy" in its true meaning.

Yoga is a very deep and complicated subject. Still, for those who are simply looking to harvest its many benefits without delving too deeply into it, the two sections of yoga that are worth focusing on are the **Pranayamas** (breathing exercises) and the *Asanas* (poses).

Some of the benefits of practicing yoga regularly are:

It is an excellent whole-body workout routine: Yoga is known to be a great whole-body workout because, unlike strength training, yoga poses focus on working out and building combined muscle groups rather than singular muscles. As a result, yoga improves strength and flexibility by forcing muscles from all around your body to work in cooperation. In addition, since a lot of yoga poses require you to work on your body balance, it is a great way to improve that aspect of your physical fitness as well.

It reduces the risk of chronic illnesses: It is said that inflammation within the body is often a cause of chronic illnesses involving organs such as the heart. Yoga is known to be beneficial in reducing inflammation and, thus, the risk of many such chronic diseases.

It helps improve mental health: Like meditation, yoga is also great at reducing stress. In addition, it also helps with many other mental health issues such as anxiety, depression, insomnia, etc. It can also help a lot in improving self-esteem and confidence, as has been proven by a lot of studies.

It helps you to perform better: Since yoga helps improve your mental and physical health, it directly affects and dramatically enhances our ability to be constantly productive at work or any other activity we engage in.

It improves sleep: Because yoga works out your physical body and helps calm your mental activity by reducing stress and anxiety, it also improves your sleep quality. Regular yoga practice can also help maintain a good sleeping schedule if you strategically time your yoga routines before and after waking up in the morning.

Improving Sleep and Stress

It's no secret that sleep directly affects your stress levels. So whether you get an adequate amount of sleep in a day or not makes a huge difference in how relaxed you are and how energetic you feel when you wake up in the morning. But getting enough sleep is not just enough; the *quality* of the sleep also matters.

The importance of getting enough sleep should not be underestimated. Scientists have demonstrated that poor sleep can directly and negatively affect hormone levels, physical performance, and cognitive ability, leading to an increased risk of gaining weight and developing health problems for adults and children.

Getting enough shut-eye can improve your health by reducing your appetite, enhancing your performance at the gym, and generally making you a more well-rounded individual. Sleep quantity and quality have dropped during the past few decades. Many people consistently have trouble sleeping. One of the most important things you can do for your health and weight is to get a good night's sleep.

Significance of bright light

Your circadian rhythm is your body's internal clock. It balances your brain, body, and hormones, keeping you alert when you need to be and signaling when it is time to sleep. Access to healthy daylight (natural sunshine or artificial sources) is essential for maintaining a normal circadian rhythm. This enhances the quality and duration of sleep, increasing alertness during the day.

Daytime exposure to bright light increased sleep quality and duration in patients with insomnia. As a result, time spent drifting to sleep was cut by an astonishing 83%. The same effect was seen in an older population when exposed to intense light throughout the day for two hours; their average sleep time increased by a massive two hours. While most studies have focused on patients with severe sleep problems, getting daily light exposure will likely assist us all. Try to spend some time outdoors in bright light each day if you can, or if you can't get enough natural light into your life, try buying a bright light device or bulbs to use too.

Exposure to evening light

In the same way that daytime sun exposure is good for you, evening light exposure is harmful. Again, this is because of how it alters your internal clock. Light can suppress melatonin and other hormones that aid in relaxation, making your body feel as though it is still daytime when it isn't. So, in the evening, try to spend a little time before bedtime in more subdued lighting and not staring at a computer screen, tablet or mobile phone. Ideally, you should switch off the TV and all bright lights at least two hours before you want to go to sleep.

Don't consume caffeine late in the day.

Caffeine is consumed by 90% of the population in the United States and the United Kingdom due to its many advantages. One dose can improve mental clarity, physical stamina, and performance in almost any sport. Caffeine is a stimulant that can be beneficial in the morning, but it can prevent your body from winding down at night if you drink it too late in the day.

One study found that caffeine consumption up to six hours before bedtime significantly reduced sleep quality. You can detect the effects of caffeine on blood pressure and heart rate for up to 8 hours after consumption. For this reason, drinking a lot of coffee after mid-afternoon is not advised, especially for those who are sensitive to caffeine or have difficulty sleeping. Drink decaf if you must have coffee in the late afternoon or evening.

Reduce irregular or long daytime naps

Occasional short 15-minute power-naps can be helpful to get you through a difficult day, especially if you haven't slept well the night before, but it's not good to sleep for too long or too often during the day. In case you were wondering, sleeping during the day can throw off your internal clock, leading to night-time insomnia.

Naps have variable effects on different people. Indeed, one study found that napping during the day made people sleepier overall. Another study found that short naps of 30 minutes or less improved cognitive performance during the day, whereas prolonged naps were detrimental to health and sleep. In contrast, research shows that those accustomed to napping during the day do not have poor sleep quality or interrupted sleep at night.

If you are struggling to get enough quality sleep, try cutting out naps completely for at least two weeks. On the other hand, if you sleep well at night and napping doesn't seem to affect that, then there is no need to worry about cutting out naps.

Fix your wake-up and sleep timings

Your body's internal clock, known as the circadian rhythm, is synchronized with the sun's rising and setting. Therefore, maintaining regular bedtimes and wake times can improve your quality of sleep over time.

Researchers found that people who had erratic sleep schedules and stayed up late on the weekends had more sleep complaints. The circadian rhythm and melatonin levels that tell your brain it's time to sleep can be disrupted by a lack of regular sleep, as shown in other studies. If you have trouble sleeping, try sticking to a regular schedule of getting up and going to bed. A few weeks from now, you might not even need an alarm, and you should fall asleep much more easily.

Optimize your bedroom environment

The bedroom significantly affects how well we sleep. Things like temperature, noise level, the brightness of outside lighting, and furniture placement can all have an impact. There have been a lot of studies showing that traffic and other forms of noise pollution can disrupt sleep and lead to serious health problems over time.

Ensure your bedroom is cool at night – you can snuggle under a warm blanket, but the air temperature should be cool to aid sleep. Limit the room's noise and light levels, or consider using a sleep mask and earplugs.

Get some comfortable sleep essentials.

Some people notice that staying in a hotel helps them to sleep better. This could be because a room's ambience and bed quality can significantly affect sleep. Consider investing in a new high-quality, comfortable mattress – after all, you spend around a third of your life in bed!

In a 28-day trial examining the effects of a new mattress, back pain was reduced by 57%, shoulder discomfort by 60%, and back stiffness by 59%. Quality of sleep also increased by 60%. Other research has shown that switching to fresh bedding can improve sleep quality, so keep those sheets nice and fresh and make sure your room feels comfortable and peaceful and is a pleasant retreat for you to unwind.

How to Benefit from Embracing Creativity

Explore your creative side

The positive effects of creativity on mental health are increasingly supported by scientific research. All sorts of artistic endeavors, from painting to gardening to party organizing, contribute to our ability to see things in a fresh light. We may use our imagination to make beautiful things, find solutions to problems, and revitalize our bodies and brains. Having a good time is good for our psyche. Creativity has been shown to boost mood, alleviate stress, and even strengthen the immune system.

When we're feeling creative, we often enter what's known as a "flow state," in which we can give our full attention to whatever we're doing. "Zoned out" is another term used to describe this state of mind. When we're on our game, we feel at peace and mindful. By putting us in a state of flow, creativity boosts our mood and gives us a sense of fulfillment.

It's about commitment

Investing time and energy into honing your creative skills is the first step in boosting your creative output. Avoid procrastinating. To improve your abilities, you should plan to do so, enlist the aid of others, and dedicate time, each week or each day, to doing so. For instance, if you're keen on painting, set aside time regularly to study the craft and hone your abilities.

Becoming expert

Pursuing expertise is one of the most fruitful avenues for expanding one's imaginative capacities. When you know a lot about a subject, you can solve difficulties in surprising or original ways. Reading about creative people and listening to them speak is one method of building expertise.

Work around the reward system

A major mental impediment to fostering creativity is the belief that curiosity is a luxury. When you're curious about something, reward yourself for your efforts rather than berating yourself. Allow yourself the time and space to learn about unfamiliar subjects. It's vital to give yourself rewards but finding ways to motivate yourself on your own is much more critical. The act of creating something new can be its own reward sometimes.

Start taking risks

To improve your creative ability, you need to take chances. Though your efforts might not always pay off, you'll be honing skills that will serve you well in the long run. For instance, presenting your work to the class could be nerve-wracking if you're taking a course in creative writing. However, the feedback you get from your peers and instructors is often quite helpful.

Become more confident

Building confidence is crucial because doubt in one's ability can stifle innovation. Take note of your development, applaud your achievements, and keep an eye out for inventive methods to reward your initiative. If you don't give yourself time to be creative, you won't get better at it. Set aside time at least once a week to work on a personal creative endeavor.

Shut the doors for negativity

To improve your creative abilities, you must rid your mind of critical or negative thoughts. See these as obstacles and make plans to go through them.

The fear of failure

Paralysis by analysis can happen when you are so afraid of failing that you don't manage to progress at all. Remembering that failing is an inevitable aspect of learning and growing is essential. You may have some temporary setbacks on your journey toward originality, but keep at it, and you will succeed.

Make a place for new ideas

The brainstorming process is widely used in both the classroom and the workplace, and for a good reason: it is an effective method for generating new ideas. It would be best if you initially refrained from being critical of yourself and other people. The first step is documenting your thoughts, ideas, questions, and potential answers. The objective is to develop as many ideas as possible in a short time. Next, you should consider elaborating and honing your thoughts. Recent studies suggest that low lighting levels can stimulate creative thinking, however counterintuitive it may sound. When it's dark

HOW TO BENEFIT FROM EMBRACING CREATIVITY

outside, it can be easier to let go of inhibitions and try new things creatively, even if they could backfire.

Give and Take

Start giving back the positivity

Philanthropy is the practice of making charitable contributions and giving back to the community. Since the beginning of our species, kindness has been an integral aspect of human culture. Giving back to the community in whatever form, from funding scientific research to giving time to people in need, is an example of philanthropy. To varying degrees, we can all make a positive difference in our surroundings and the world. Giving to others can be done on a small or large scale, which is part of its appeal. For example, helping a neighbor out involves as little as carrying groceries to their house.

The significance of giving

Giving back to your community by volunteering at a local organization, school, homeless shelter, animal shelter, etc., is a great way to make a difference. Investing your time in others can profoundly impact their lives, so it is critical to select a cause you care about if you are going to devote some time to it. In addition, volunteering is an excellent approach to widening one's worldview by helping those around oneself.

It can be gratifying to become a part of a community and associate with people who share your passion for change in a particular area. Serving others gives you a sense of fulfillment that might permeate other parts of your life. Your neighborhood will benefit, of course! Many of the community events and services we take for granted wouldn't exist if not for the efforts of dedicated volunteers. Volunteering at a local shelter or food bank is a great way to help those in need in your community.

Doing good deeds for the people and places you call home can help bring people together and heal rifts in the social, economic, and political spheres.

Giving back to your community by helping people in need is rewarding on many levels. Studies have shown that people who regularly volunteer have fewer health problems of every kind. And so, not surprisingly, volunteering has been linked to improved health and longevity. Not only can helping others improve your health, but it can also provide a sense of positive fulfillment. There is no greater sense of satisfaction than that which comes from helping others and making a positive difference in the world.

Volunteering is a beautiful opportunity to meet interesting people in your area and to expand your social circle. By joining forces with other people who share your interest in making the world a better place, you can quickly increase the size of your social circle. It will also assist you in comprehending the predicaments of others in your society. Being an effective and empathic citizen helps to have a broad and accepting view of the world, which ultimately leads to less feeling of frustration and more satisfaction.

Volunteering can help you develop more than just people skills. Volunteering teaches you compassion, perseverance, and tolerance. Working with a wide group of individuals can help you grow as a communicator and in many other ways that will serve you well in the future.

How should you start?

Here are a few easy methods to start making a difference in people's lives and giving back to the community.

Start with donating time

Giving back to your community by volunteering at a local organization, school, homeless shelter, animal shelter, etc, is a great way to make a difference. Investing your time in others can have a profound impact on their lives.

Act of kindness could be random

An act of kindness like helping a neighbor move some heavy furniture or carrying bags of groceries is appreciated and remembered. The old adage about doing a good deed every day still holds true.

Support a child

To make a difference in the life of a child in foster care, consider volunteering with an organization like Together We Rise. They welcome volunteers from around the United States and offer assistance to young people who have aged out of the foster care system. Alternatively, you could ask your local school if there are any volunteering opportunities.

Support the senior communities

Some seniors avoid feelings of loneliness by attending a local senior center – you can often volunteer at these centers. Alternatively, you can help by doing chores for older adults, so they can continue living alone and comfortably in their own homes. Volunteering with groups that aim to aid the elderly is another way to assist those seniors in need.

Go green

In this age of rapidly increasing air pollution, trees are more important than ever, not just for the planet. Trees remove carbon dioxide from the air, release water, and take it in, all while producing oxygen. Each tree we plant serves many purposes: decreasing pollution while fostering biodiversity and improving human health. You can volunteer to plant trees or maintain trees and woodlands.

Recycle

Helping to make the most of our planet's natural resources and reduce pollution by recycling can feel particularly rewarding. In addition, making money by trading in recyclable plastics at the local recycling facility is a nice bonus for recycling.

There are many ways to give back to your community, such as recycling and volunteering. Take some time to think about what you care about, get stuck, and start making a difference.

What Difference do People (and Animals) Make?

Keeping the right company

The people you surround yourself with have an incredible impact on your personality, your behavior, your thoughts, and in turn, your overall life. Not everyone in your life is here to stay, and it is up to you to decide who eventually does.

The right company can be crucial in improving your overall lifestyle and mental health. Positive people spread positivity around them, and negative people do the opposite. When you surround yourself with negative people, you are more likely to be stressed. On the contrary, positive people will motivate you to rise up every time you feel low, support you in your endeavors, and help you when in need.

There are three groups of people that usually matter most to men.

Family

Family is the gift we have been given since birth. We don't get to choose our family, but those who are blessed with an understanding and supportive family know that no other group of people is more reliable in your life.

Most families, like most individuals, are not exactly perfect. No family is free from occasional quarrels and disagreements, but what matters is that they stick with each other despite such occurrences.

Unfortunately for many, however, family can be much more difficult. Dysfunctional families that bring people down rather than support them are not difficult to find in our society. And sometimes, putting some distance between yourself and your family instead of letting yourself be impacted can be the better solution for your mental health and psyche.

However, if you have a family that cares about you, treasure them and spend time with them. Support them and help them, and you'll find that they'll do the same for you.

Friends and co-workers

Unlike family, we choose who we call our friends. We meet people, talk with them, and if we enjoy each other's company, we call ourselves friends. Some people are more outgoing and like to have many friends, while others prefer having fewer friends they can trust completely. Either way, friends are a great resource to have.

Find a community

The health risk of our increasingly interconnected and individualistic modern lives is loneliness, which has been dubbed "the new smoking." Mental wellbeing can suffer rapidly from isolation. We are hardwired to seek out and thrive in connections with others, and these bonds protect us from loneliness. Having a group of trusted friends by your side as you experience the highs and lows of life can do wonders for your confidence.

Sharing hobbies and interests with someone can have an incredible effect on your mental health. Sharing your life experiences with them over a cup of tea, or a can of beer is simply one of the best ways to vent some stress and find enjoyment in the chaos of life.

Since you have the freedom to choose your friends, make sure to do that wisely. Keep friends who care about you and help you close. Treat them the same as you would like them to treat you. Good friends can last a lifetime, so keep that in mind and hang out with them when you can!

While you cannot precisely choose your co-workers, you can at least choose who you want to maintain a professional relationship with and who you want to become friends with. It's not uncommon to make friends with your co-workers, but remember that, ultimately, they are people you work with. This means that unless you are certain of their character, you should probably avoid oversharing about your life with them and maintain a certain professional etiquette even as friends.

Romantic partners

Having someone with whom you can share everything about your life is amazing. Being in love is one of the most euphoric feelings in the world. However, it is easy to get blinded by that feeling and forget about the things that matter to us. Unfortunately, like almost any other relationship in our lives, romantic relationships are seldom perfect. It's not just women who get backed into a toxic relationship that they can't find their way out of. This happens to many men as well. Finding someone who you are comfortable and compatible with is the key to avoiding such situations.

When it comes to finding a potential romantic partner, many try to overcompensate for their flaws and are not completely honest with their partner at the outset. This can result in problems in the future because of expectations from that partner that they cannot meet. This is why honesty is one of the most essential things in a relationship.

Apart from honesty, below are a few other requirements for a healthy romantic relationship with anyone.

Trust

Trust is, of course, another thing that is absolutely necessary for a healthy relationship. Mutual trust means you can share anything with your partner and know they feel the same. Trusting each other does not necessarily mean that you both share every little detail, but it does mean that neither of you is worried about the things you don't know. You know these things will not affect your relationship or feelings for each other.

Personal space

Another crucial element to any healthy and successful relationship is respect for each other's personal space. Being in a relationship doesn't mean people do not need their "alone time." On the contrary, everyone needs their personal space; when they begin to lose it, they may feel cornered and suffocated. Respect each other's privacy and personal space, and you'll find you're much happier when you're together.

Mutual respect

This is another quite obvious one. Mutual respect is essential in a healthy relationship. This is, in fact, true for every other relationship and not just for romantic relationships. Respect for each other means that you recognize them for who they are and accept them into your life. If you can feel your respect dwindling, try being curious. When we first meet people, we are often very interested in who they are, their likes and dislikes, and what makes them tick. Try rekindling this curiosity and asking questions to learn more about your partner or anyone in your life; you might find that it brings a new level of respect to the relationship.

Enjoy each other's company

When it comes to romance, perhaps the most important thing is that you enjoy each other's company. Enjoying each other's company means you're comfortable with each other no matter what. If you have to go out of your way to feel happy when being with your partner, it might be an indication that there's a lack of compatibility. Truly compatible people can sit in silence beside each other, enjoy themselves, and be at peace.

Sometimes when we are single, we long to find a romantic partner and can tend to settle for second best. Try to be clear in your mind about what is important to you, and don't compromise when dating because if you do, you are likely to find yourself attached to someone who ultimately isn't right for you. It is well worth waiting for your perfect match to come along. Patience and learning to be comfortable being single are the key things that will bring you success here.

Find your fun and funny

The ability to laugh at yourself, and together as partners, is often cited as critical in maintaining mental health and fostering resilience. Spending time being goofy and lighthearted together can relieve stress, promote good mental health and strengthen your relationship. On the other hand, when taken to extremes, seriousness can lead to cynicism, jadedness, and hyper-criticism.

Pets

People with pets are everywhere on every social media platform nowadays. They post their pets eating, sleeping, playing, and doing anything and everything. But have you noticed something? In most of these videos, the owners of the pets are happy and having fun.

You might think of pets as just another form of entertainment, but they can profoundly impact your mental health and well-being. So this might be your cue to get a pet today if you haven't got one already. There are various ways in which pets can help improve our physical, social, and mental health.

The challenges of keeping a pet

Although keeping a pet can be a bit difficult since you have to pay attention to them, feed them, care for them, etc, for many people, the benefits far outweigh the challenges. But when it comes to owning a pet, there are some ground rules that all pet owners know and respect.

1. If you cannot take care of a pet, don't keep it. Pets deserve a healthy lifestyle as well. People who cannot afford to feed their pet or cannot

provide what the animal needs to thrive should not simply keep a pet just for their benefit.
2. Adopting a pet is almost always a better alternative than buying. Many organizations help animals in need find suitable homes, and many do not even charge for you to take a pet home.
3. Adopt pets that can adapt to your environment. While many pets can survive in most environments where we live, some are much more inclined towards hotter or colder climates and may find it difficult to thrive if forced to live elsewhere. Proper research about your animal before you decide to keep it is essential.'

Why get a pet?

If you feel comfortable that you could keep a pet and help it to thrive, then here are a few reasons why pets are so great for you if you're trying to build a healthier lifestyle.

They help with depression

Pets can help with depression, anxiety, and stress. Pets are also wonderful for loneliness, grief, and dementia. They can even help you cope with PTSD or autism!

They foster social interaction.

Pets are a fabulous way to improve your social life. They can help you meet new people, and they're great for ensuring you have enough time in the day to spend with family members or friends. The best part about pets is that they're always there for us when we need them! Treat them right, and they will more than reciprocate those feelings towards you.

They encourage us to be active

If you have an active pet like a dog, you will probably get much more physical exercise than you bargained for. This is because pets encourage you to go out on walks, play with them, and be active around them, thus improving your physical health quite effectively.

Consulting a therapist

The things discussed, such as exercise, a regular sleep schedule, healthy diets, and social engagements, are essential for a healthy lifestyle, but sometimes, they aren't enough. With mental health issues such as depression and anxiety on a constant rise, professional help has also become quite a necessity in such cases.

There's still quite a bit of stigma attached to consulting a therapist, and there are people who feel like they might get shunned or made fun of for doing so, but there's really nothing wrong with it. There's no shame in admitting that we are not perfect – none of us are. And if a consultation with a professional can help you become happier and find answers to the questions in your life, then it seems wise to let them.

Professionals such as therapists and psychiatrists undergo training to help people going through challenging times; thus, they have the knowledge to provide insight and guide us through them.

When to get professional help

It's never a bad idea to consult a therapist when you find yourself stressed, but there are certain situations when it is the best solution and where trying to handle everything on your own can be the worst decision you can take.

Emotional instability

Emotional instability can be caused by many things in life, such as a relationship breakup, loss of a job, a significant career setback, diagnosis of a major disease or illness, and so on. During such times, a therapist can help you find the right outlook on your life to face your issues, deal with them, and overcome them.

Another prominent reason for emotional instability or distress is losing someone near and dear, which will always be a difficult experience, no matter who we are and how much experience we may have in life. During such times, especially if we don't have anyone we want to offload to and share the grief with, a therapist can help vent out the flurry of emotions and feelings that get built up inside us.

Addictions

Trying to handle addictions by yourself can backfire severely. Addiction comes in several phases. In the first phase, people refuse to recognize their addiction as a problem. However, when they recognize it in the later stages, people often make the mistake of thinking they can take care of it by themselves. Receiving help from a therapist in such situations can help avoid falling further down the rabbit hole and get rid of the problem as soon as possible.

Mental disorders

Mental disorders are serious issues and should be treated as such. Disorders like chronic depression, schizophrenia, bipolar disorders, post-traumatic stress disorder, and so on absolutely require the help of a trained medical professional. Proper medical evaluation is only the first step, and an essential one, towards recognizing the crux of the problem and treating it.

Do it Your Way!

Break the rules

Human beings are said to be social animals. We like being around others and depend on each other to achieve specific goals in life. Over the years, we have become what we call a "society," and society has rules. These are rules that we have all mutually agreed upon, to some degree or other. For example, we believe that harming others, especially for our benefit, is wrong. We believe that helping others and contributing to society is good. But amongst these sets of rules, many can be unnecessary or even detrimental to our happiness and well-being.

Who was it that decided men can't wear pink? Who said skincare is only for women? There's nothing wrong with spending some money on yourself occasionally if you're broke. Likewise, there's nothing shameful in asking for help at work when you're lagging behind.

These societal rules do not particularly benefit anyone, but people still like to hold onto them to feel like a part of our society. BREAK THOSE RULES. Do what makes you happy. Not everybody has to be the same. Your unique tastes, life principles, beliefs, etc, are all part of you and your personality. They make you who you are. Of course, when breaking the rules, it's also important to understand where to draw the line; the key thing is to try to break free from peer pressure and tread your own path.

Oscar Wilde's famous quote, "Be yourself, everyone else is taken", isn't just a cute saying on a T-shirt. There's quite a lot of truth to it. Being capable of independent thinking is one of the most amazing superpowers we've been given, and there's no reason for you not to be you. Embrace your uniqueness and live true to it. Not everything in life needs validation. Be quirky and unique; ultimately, the world will see you for who you are. People who manage to free themselves like this tend to report feeling much more content.

Trust your gut

It is said that the gut contains more than 100 million neurons and has a separate secondary nervous system that is called the enteric nervous system. It's sometimes even called a "second brain" by medical professionals. So, when people say you should trust your gut, you should probably take their advice.

If you have an internal feeling or an intuition, do not be quick to dismiss it. Our intuition is built upon the knowledge we have subconsciously acquired through all our experiences in life. Learn to trust yourself and your instincts rather than giving in to the advice and suggestions of other people. Independent thinking is what we humans are best at, yet we often let our thoughts get influenced and clouded by what is around us.

Confidence

One of the most essential qualities to have to live a healthy, happy, and satisfactory lifestyle is confidence. It is the feeling that you can do something or know about something without any doubt, and it gives you the ability to take the steps that you need to take to achieve success in whatever field you want to be successful.

Self-confidence is a powerful tool that helps us through difficult times in our lives. It gives us hope and helps us get back on track to fulfilling our dreams and desires. Without confidence, people fall into self-doubt and end up doubting everything about themselves, which results in mental conditions such as imposter syndrome and inferiority complex.

We all struggle with self-confidence at one point or another in our lives. We will find ourselves doubting the quality of our work, the people we love, whether we've made the right decision, or whether we are good enough for this job, good enough for love, and so on. During these times, self-confidence plays a crucial role in what happens to us next and how we cope with it.

Our parents, teachers, and friends often tell us how to be confident when they see that we lack it. But self-confidence is a state of mind that you cannot force; it has to come naturally. Furthermore, we must realize that we can only get self-confidence if we genuinely believe in ourselves. And hence, the best and the most effective method to build confidence is to change your perspective and mindset. Here are a few tips that will help you do that, thus boosting your self-confidence.

Set achievable goals

So often, people make the mistake of being overconfident just before losing that confidence. It happens to everyone. Sometimes you think that you can get this task done within 10 minutes, but to your surprise, it's been 30 minutes, and you still can't get it done. So you lose confidence, leave it be, and return to your shell. Instead, try setting achievable goals and seeing them through. If you're new at something, start really small. Accomplishing numerous smaller goals is much more satisfying than trying your hand at a huge plan and not being able to see it through.

Measure yourself with realistic standards

Another similar mistake that many people make is they judge themselves too harshly. In this age of social media and the internet, everyone you know seems to be doing so well in their life. But remember that people only show better views of their life to outsiders. Everyone is still struggling in their life with something or other. So, ensure you don't measure yourself against unrealistic standards because doing so doesn't have any benefits.

Imperfection is beauty

While seeking perfection in what you do can encourage you to do better and improve yourself, chasing perfection too much can also lead to a loss of self-confidence. Understanding the beauty in imperfection is something that comes naturally, but it is important, nonetheless. So here's something to think about if you are someone who chases perfection in everything – If everything in the world was perfect, wouldn't it just be plain, simple, and boring?

Understand yourself and your priorities

Your priorities define a core part of your personality and deeply connect with the quality of your "self-confidence." People who have low self-confidence are not lacking it entirely. When it comes to something that really matters to them, you will find them standing their ground no matter what. Understanding your priorities and accepting them gives you the ability to be confident in your choices and decisions and thus helps you improve your self-confidence.

Embrace your failures

Everyone fails. The more a person seems successful to you, the more likely they have been through more failures to achieve that success. It happens to everyone, not just you. So, learn to embrace your failures – they are definitely not a reason you should feel embarrassed or scared to try new things. Own them, learn from them, and keep pushing your way in because if you let your failures control you, you'll always remain a failure. Treat them as nothing but stepping-stones in your path to success.

Seek out positive people

We have already seen how positive people can help you stay in the right mindset, which is also true for your self-confidence. One of the best ways to boost your self-confidence is to get positive affirmations from the people around you. For example, when someone praises you or is thankful to you for doing something for them, it gives you an immense sense of achievement.

Remember to simply say 'thank you' when someone praises something about you or something you have done. We tend to be bashful and try to diminish being praised. Not only can that feel quite unpleasant to the person giving the praise, but it also makes the praise less rewarding for you. If you tend to do this, make a commitment today to simply smile and say 'thank you' when someone gives you recognition or praise.

Embrace your "Alone Time"

Everyone needs some alone time, whether it's to recharge their batteries or just to get away from the noise and distractions of life. We can use the time that we spend alone with ourselves in any way. Of course, some people prefer focusing on hobbies, while others may enjoy relaxing. But for all of us, there are times when we think – "I wish I were somewhere alone."

The problem with always being around other people is that their needs can take precedence over yours, which can be frustrating. For example, you want to spend your time with your friends and family, but they're always involved in something or other that requires their attention. And if you try to take a break from them, they might feel you're avoiding or ignoring them! So what should you do? How should you spend your free time when you have so many options?

Well, the answer is simple: spend more time alone. In fact, according to a new study published in The Journal of Social Psychology by researchers at the University of California (UC), spending time alone has been linked with better physical health outcomes and less anxiety than spending time with others.

1. Alone time is healthy. Studies show that it's important to have alone time to maintain your well-being and mental health. For example, a study by the University of Michigan found that "people who had more than four hours of solo activity per day were much less likely to develop depression."

2. Alone time allows us to think independently and creatively. When we're not distracted by our surroundings or other people, we can let our minds wander and develop new ideas for projects. By taking a little bit of time each day for solitude, you'll be more creative than ever!

3. Alone time helps us learn better ways of interacting with others and ourselves! When we're not distracted by others, we have the chance to reflect on what we've learned in our lives so far and use this reflection as motivation for change to continue to improve our future lives.

How do you know when you need some time alone?

Believe it or not, our body and mind give us signals when we have just about had enough of people around us and want some solitude. As a result, our moods start to change, and we end up behaving irrationally or abnormally.

Have you ever found yourself becoming irritable? That's your mind telling you that whatever it is – you've probably had enough of it. That's when you want to be left alone. Do you sometimes feel overburdened and overwhelmed by whatever is happening around you? Alone time can probably help!

Pay attention to these shifts in your behavioral patterns and your feelings, and try to find somewhere secluded for yourself during such times.

Make your own destiny

The saying, "You make your own destiny," means that your future is determined by the choices you make and not outside forces. The phrase comes from Latin, "Faber est suae quisque fortunae." which literally means "every man makes his own fortune." It is one of the most popular Latin phrase tattoos.

The phrase is a call to action for you to be confident about yourself and take bold steps to gain control of your life. In other words, it reminds us that we are in charge of our future and should not let others tell us what to do. However, it also means that if you don't take care of yourself physically or emotionally, you will have difficulty getting what you want out of life.

In this present day, not everyone is born with the same privileges. Some people have the luxury of choosing what they want to do and pursuing their dreams with all the help they need. But unfortunately, many people still have to struggle but manage to reach their goals and become happy with themselves.

Our society is diverse, and this makes us better as a whole, but many people have significant challenges to overcome before fulfilling their passions in life. Use people who have struggled and achieved as your inspiration - seek them out and learn from them.

Feeling confident in yourself and how you are living your life is crucial. Some people may try to tear you down, but if you know what's best for you and how to take care of yourself, nothing is stopping you from being successful. We live in a world where people can create their destinies. With a little effort and focus, you can design your life as you want it and this is what we should all strive for.

And Finally

Amazon review

If you enjoyed this book, please take a few moments to write a review of it on the Amazon product page. It only takes a few seconds and it helps me a lot. Thank you!

https://www.amazon.com/dp/B0BFC3CXLS

Printed in Great Britain
by Amazon